FIRST GRAPHICS

SEASONS

SPRING IS SPECIAL

BY CARI MEISTER

ILLUSTRATED BY
JIM LINGENFELTER

CAPSTONE PRESS
a capstone imprint

First Graphics are published by Capstone Press,
151 Good Counsel Drive, P.O. Box 669, Mankato, Minnesota 56002.
www.capstonepub.com

Printed in the United States of America in Stevens Point, Wisconsin.

032010
005741WZF10

Books published by Capstone Press are manufactured with paper containing at least 10 percent post-consumer waste.

Library of Congress Cataloging-in-Publication Data

Meister, Cari.
Spring is special / by Cari Meister ; illustrated by Jim Lingenfelter.
p. cm.
Includes index.
ISBN 978-1-4296-4729-8 (library binding)
ISBN 978-1-4296-5621-4 (paperback)
1. Spring—Juvenile literature. I. Lingenfelter, Jim, ill. II. Title.

QB637.5.M45 2011 2010000047
508.2—dc22

Editor: **Shelly Lyons**
Designer: **Alison Thiele**
Art Director: **Nathan Gassman**
Production Specialist: **Laura Manthe**

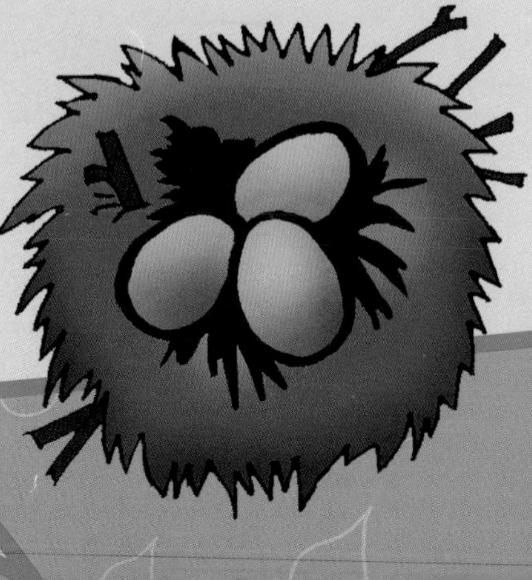

TABLE OF CONTENTS

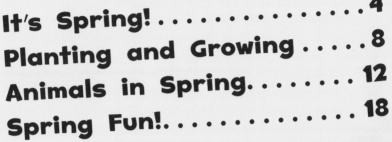

IT'S SPRING!

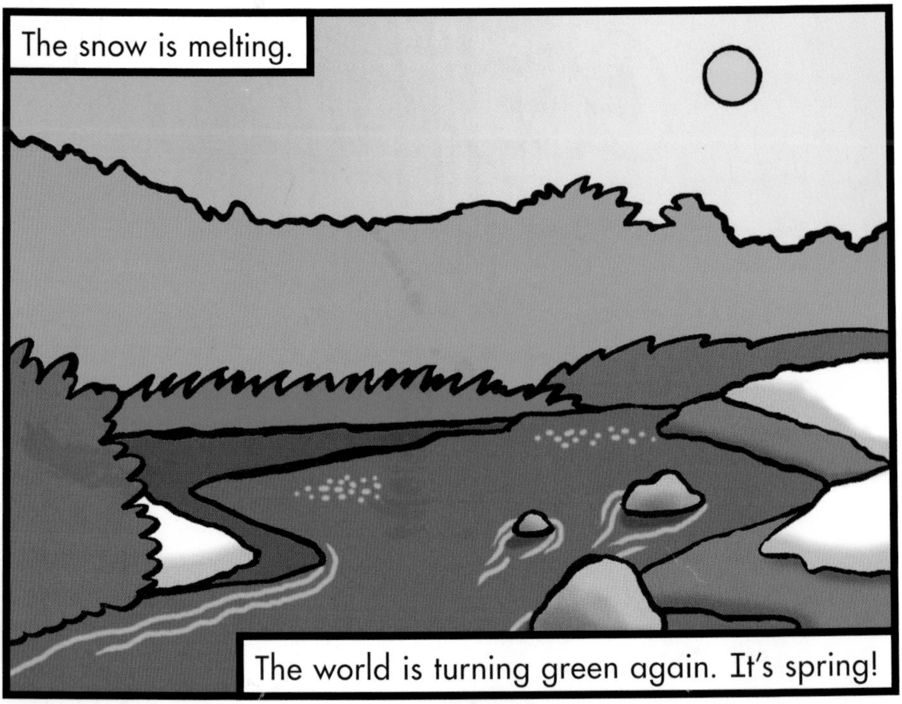
The snow is melting.
The world is turning green again. It's spring!

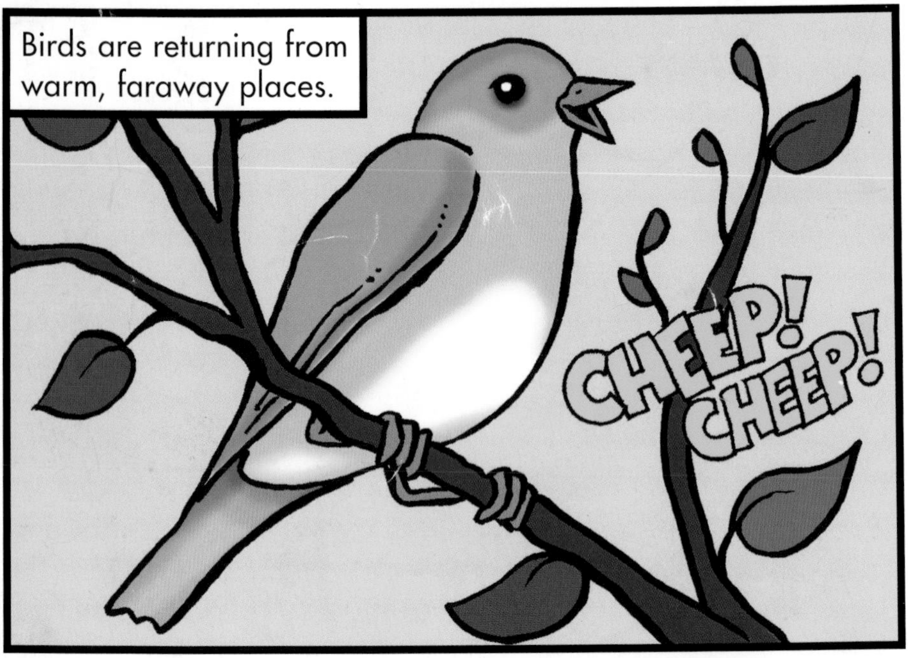
Birds are returning from warm, faraway places.
CHEEP! CHEEP!

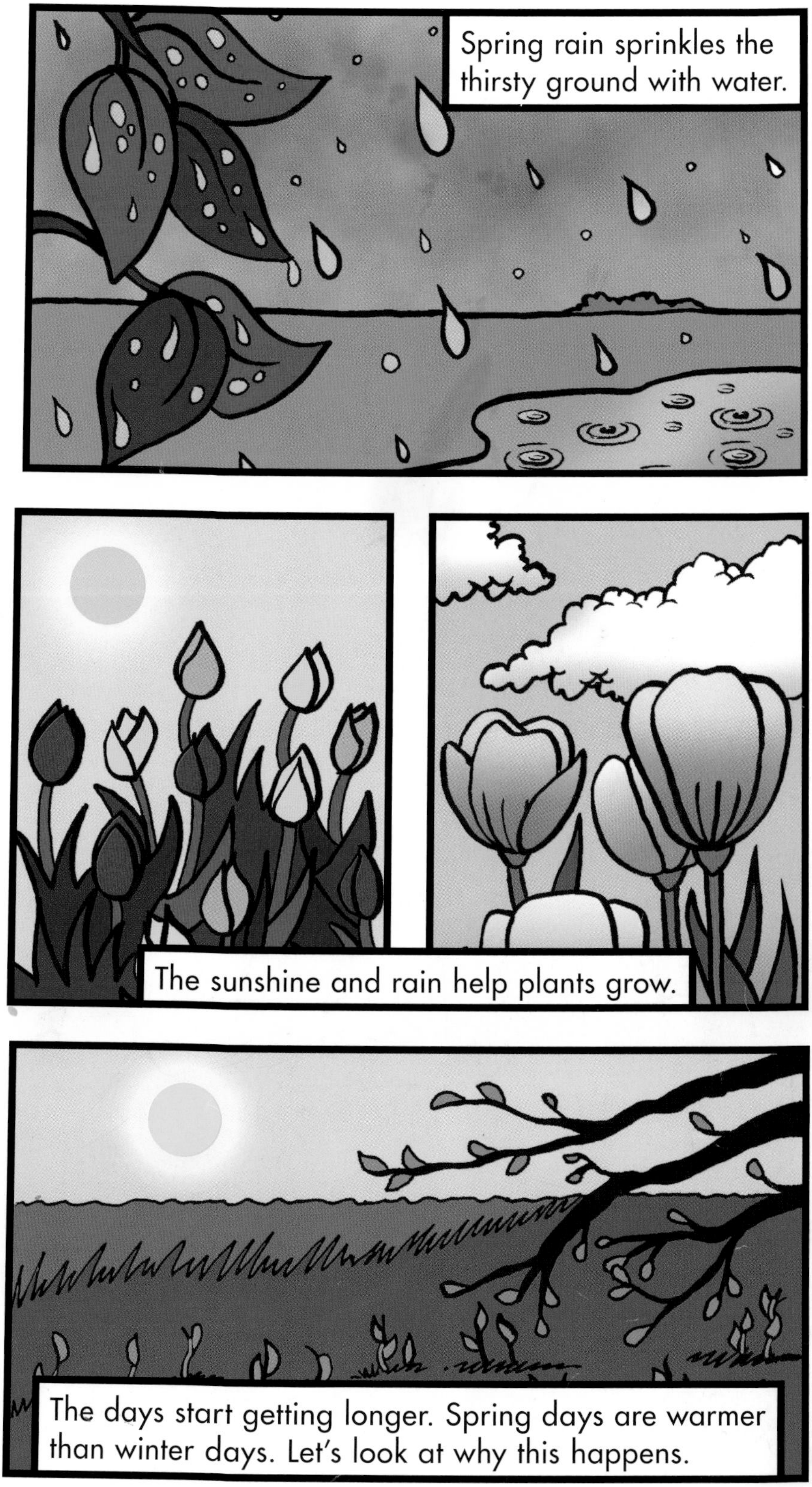
Spring rain sprinkles the thirsty ground with water.
The sunshine and rain help plants grow.
The days start getting longer. Spring days are warmer than winter days. Let's look at why this happens.

Earth is always tilted at the same angle. It moves around the sun once in a year. As Earth moves, it spins on its axis.

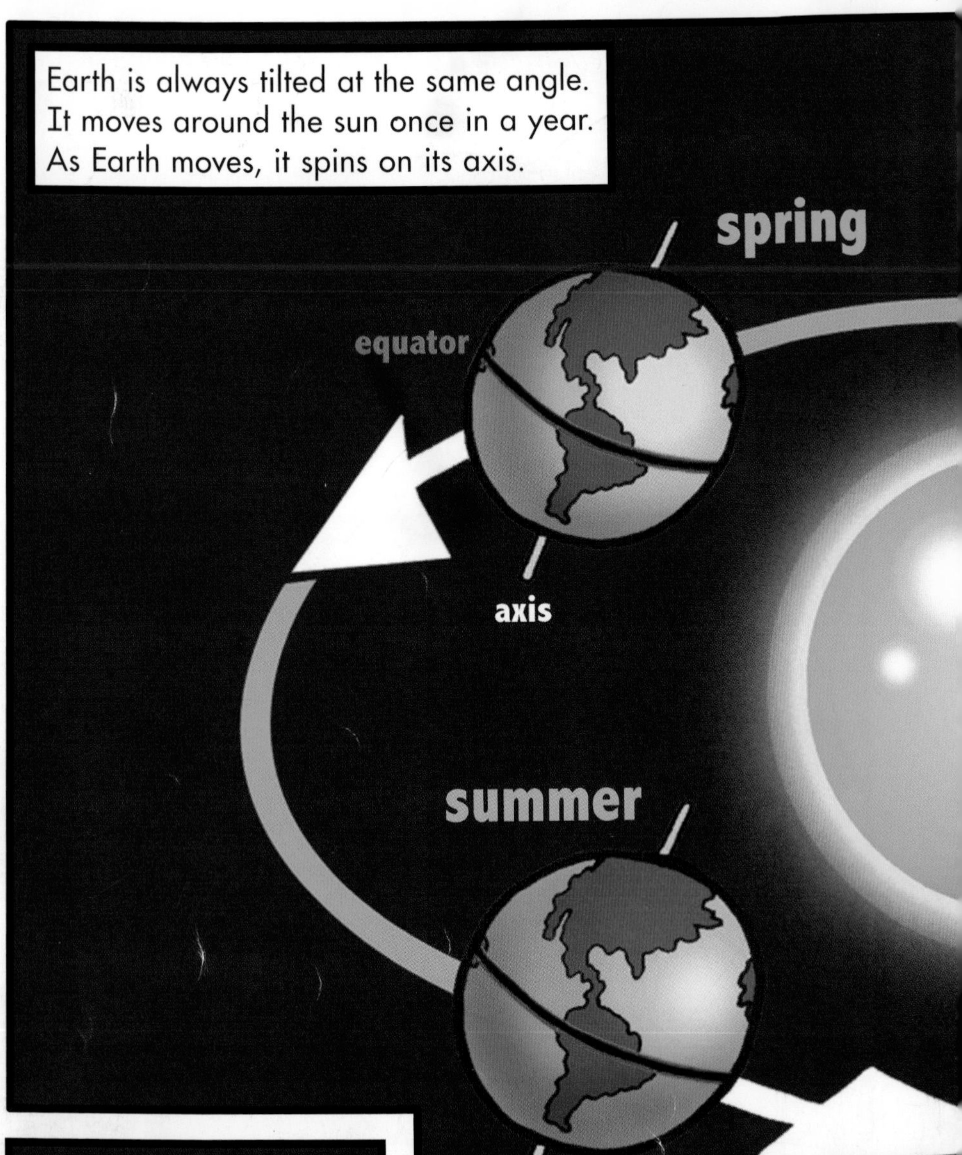
spring
equator
axis
summer

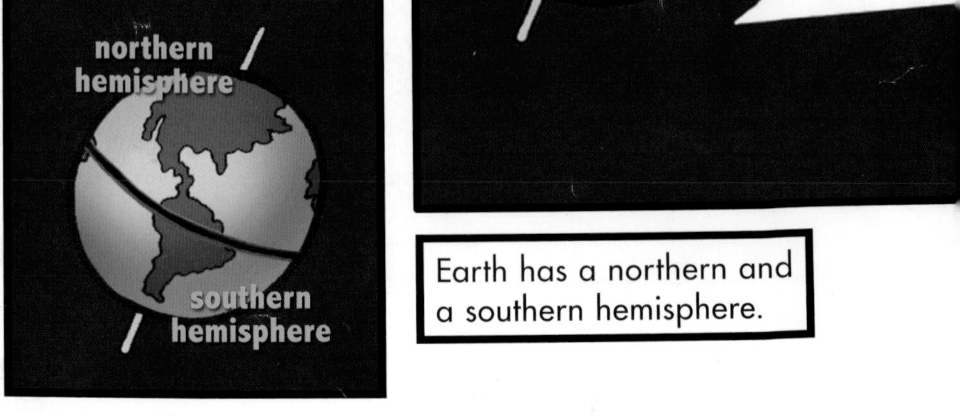
northern hemisphere
southern hemisphere

Earth has a northern and a southern hemisphere.

Northern Hemisphere Seasons

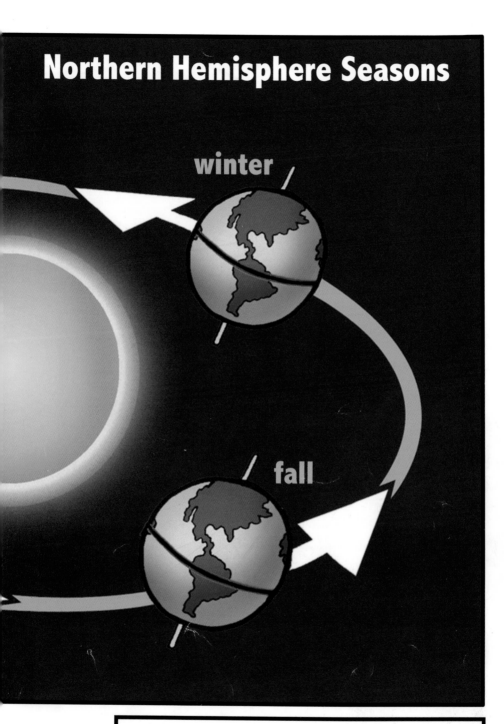

winter

fall

Each hemisphere points toward the sun at opposite times of the year. When starting to point toward the sun, a hemisphere experiences spring.

PLANTING AND GROWING

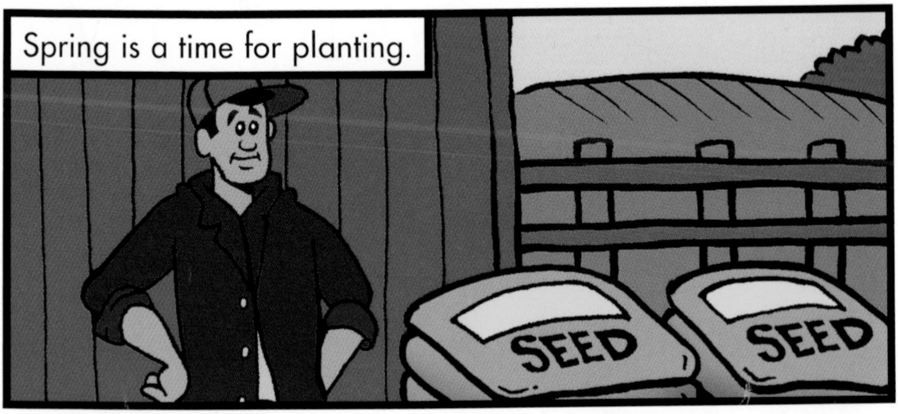
Spring is a time for planting.
SEED
SEED

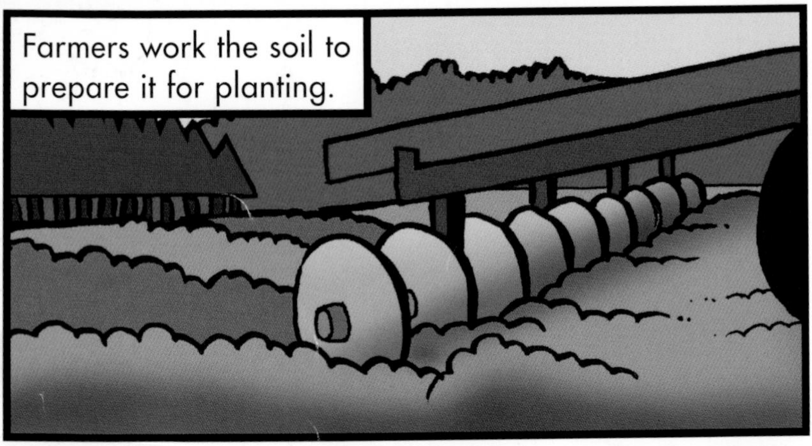
Farmers work the soil to prepare it for planting.

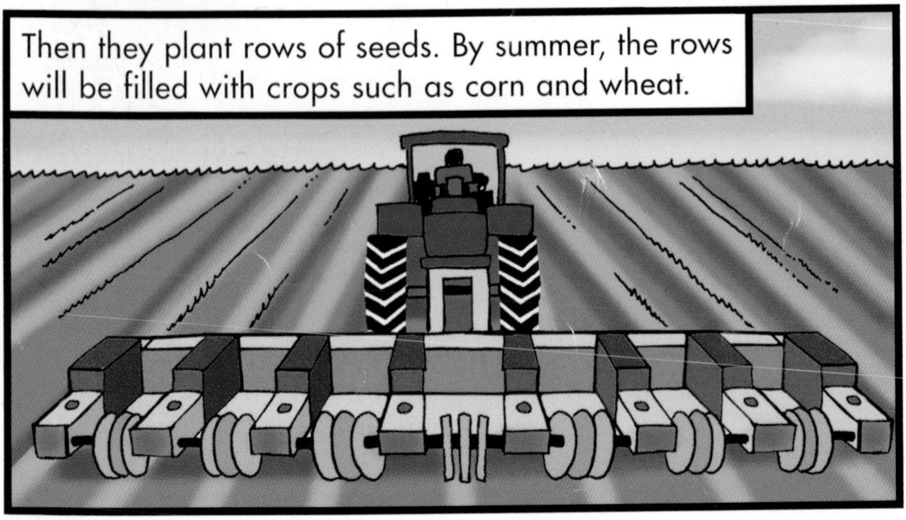
Then they plant rows of seeds. By summer, the rows will be filled with crops such as corn and wheat.

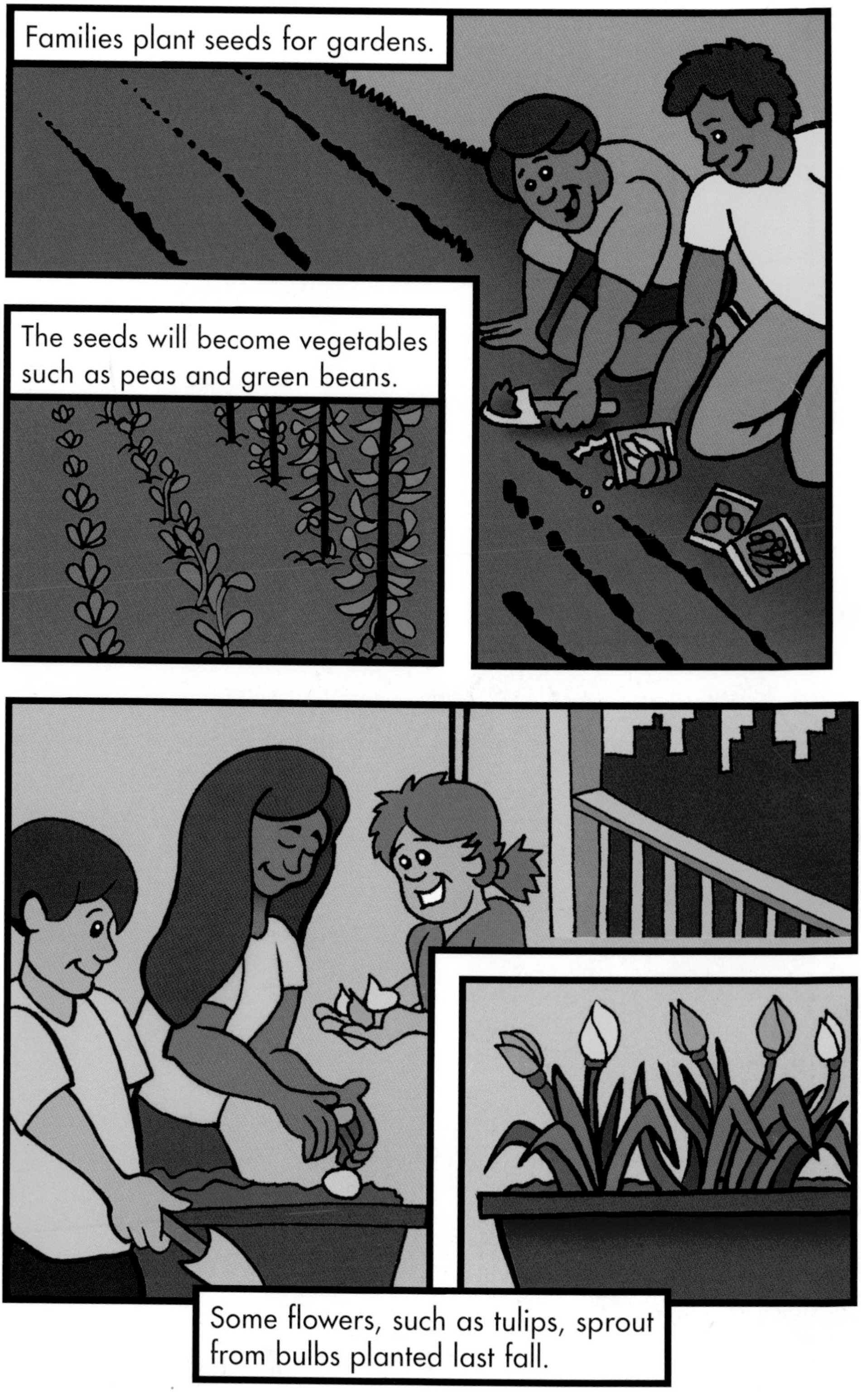
Families plant seeds for gardens.
The seeds will become vegetables such as peas and green beans.
Some flowers, such as tulips, sprout from bulbs planted last fall.

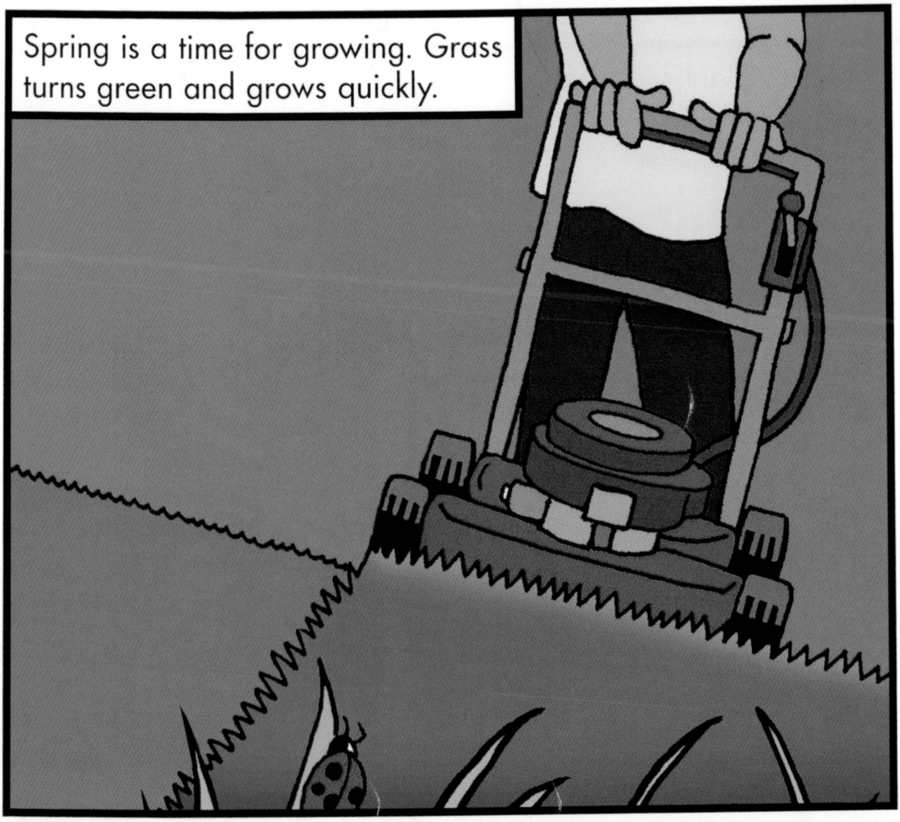
Spring is a time for growing. Grass turns green and grows quickly.

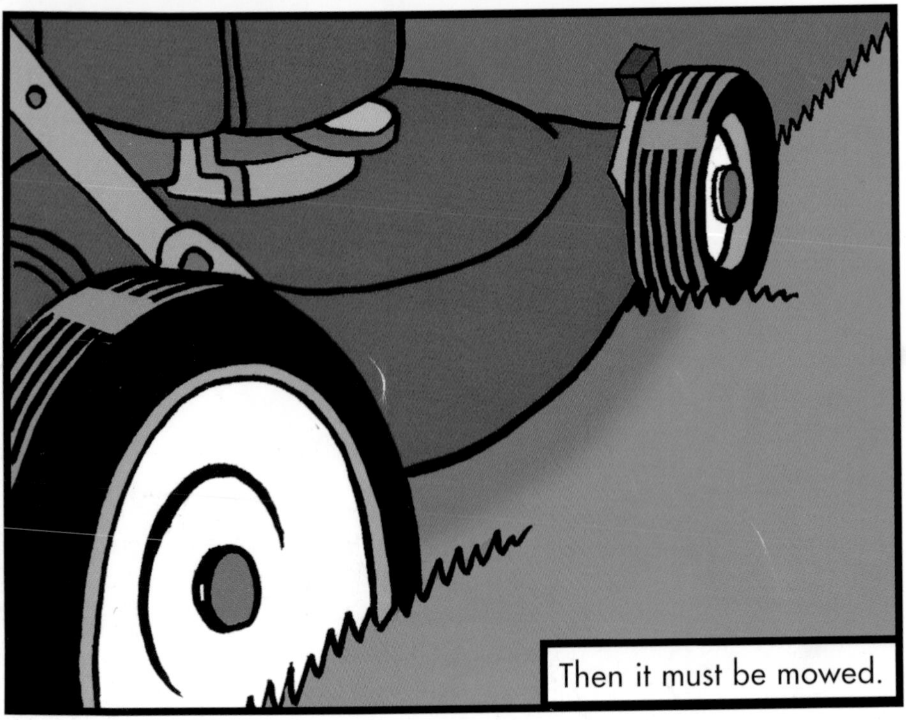
Then it must be mowed.

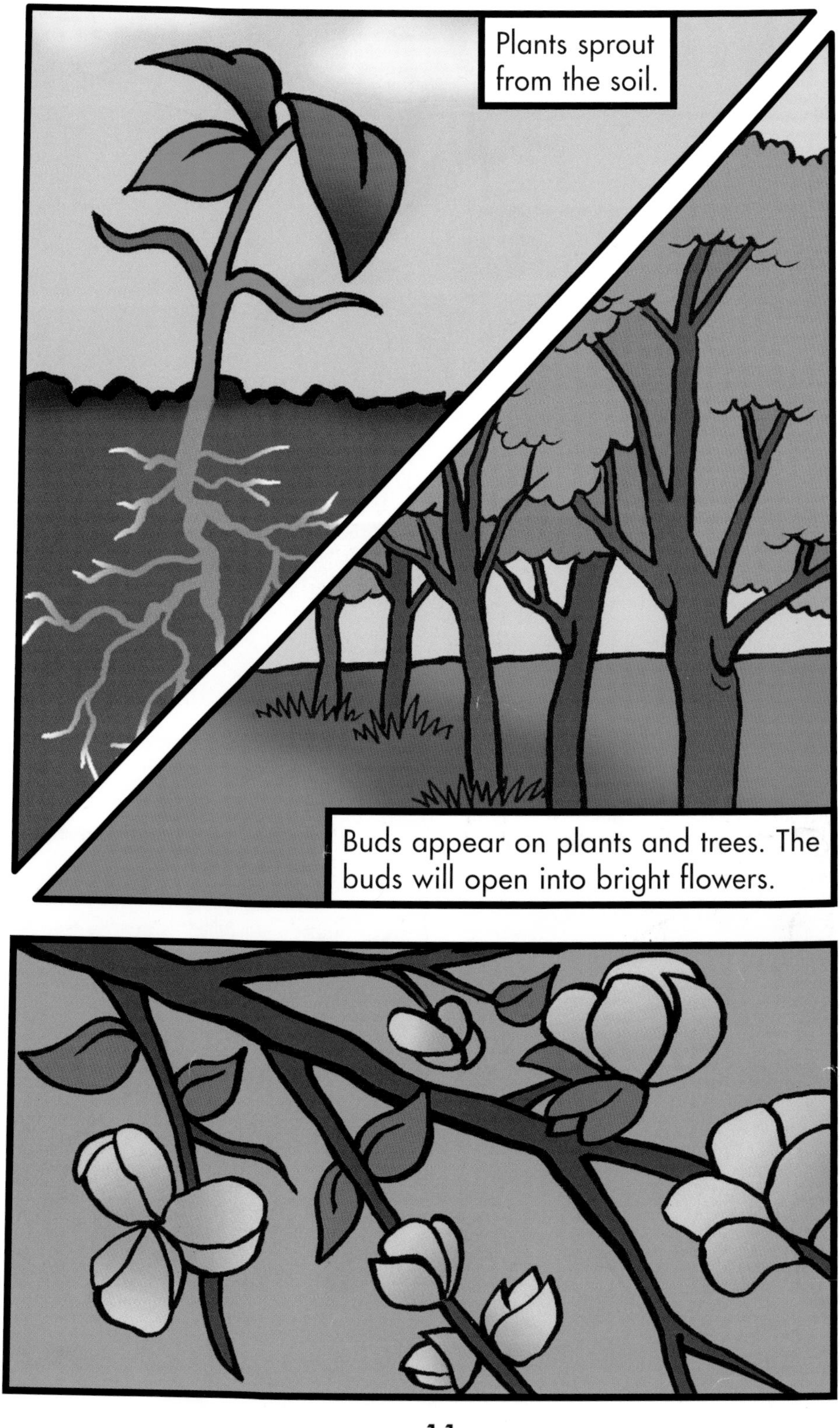
Plants sprout from the soil.
Buds appear on plants and trees. The buds will open into bright flowers.

Animals in Spring

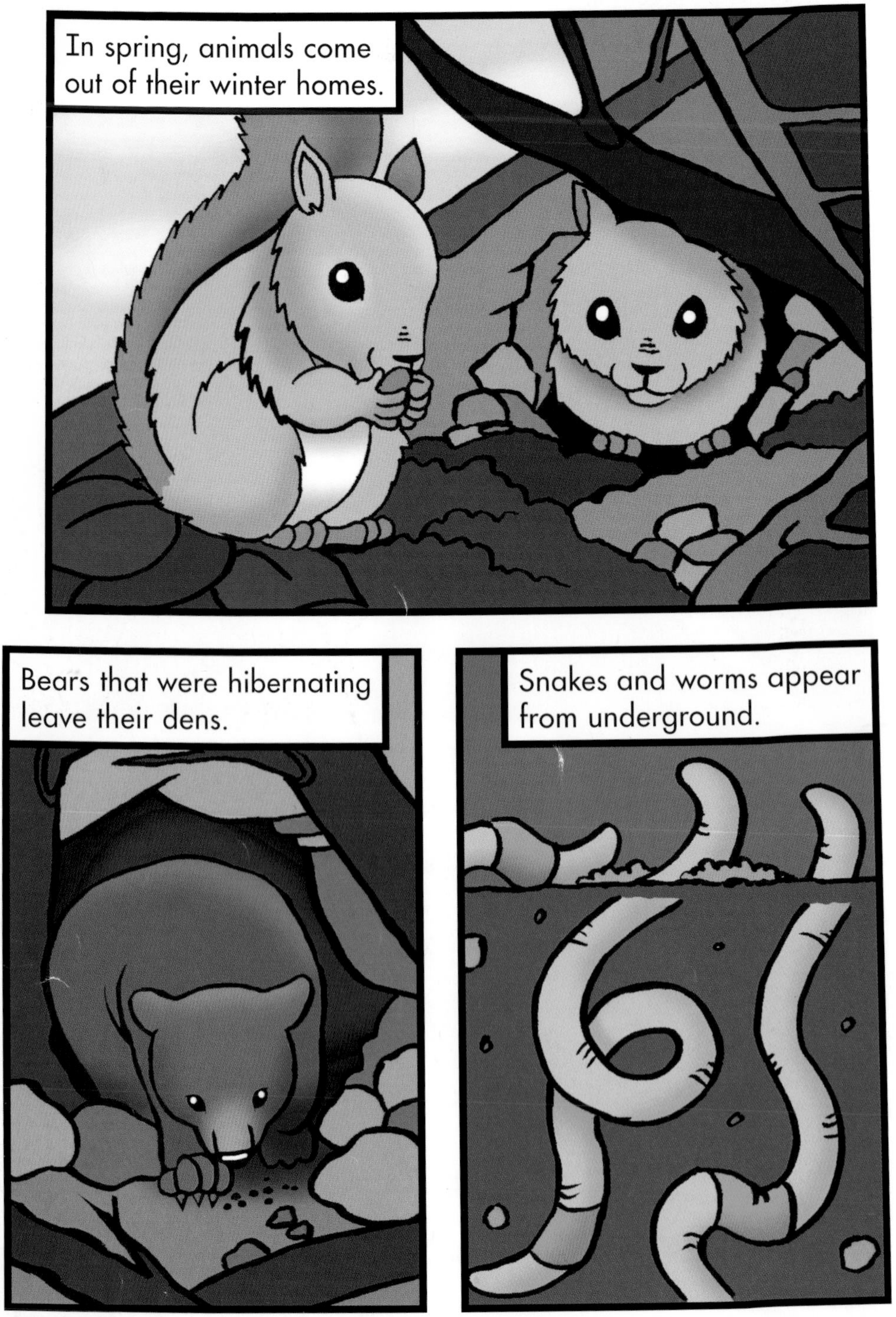
In spring, animals come out of their winter homes.
Bears that were hibernating leave their dens.
Snakes and worms appear from underground.

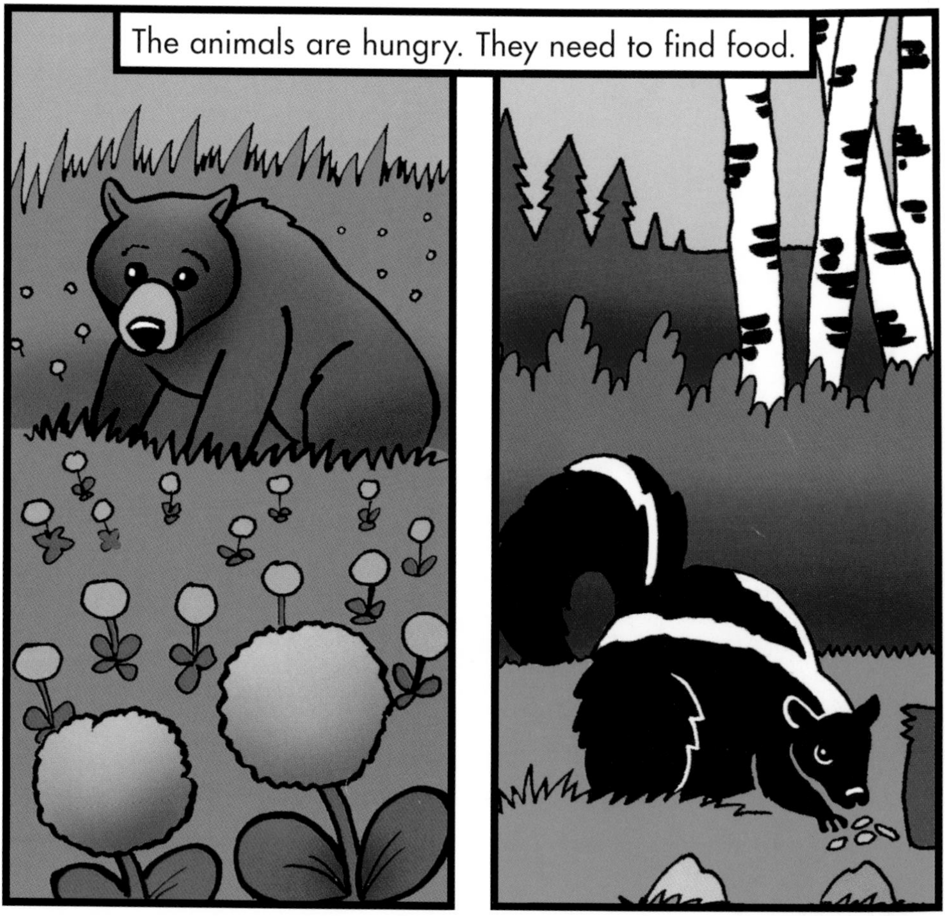
The animals are hungry. They need to find food.

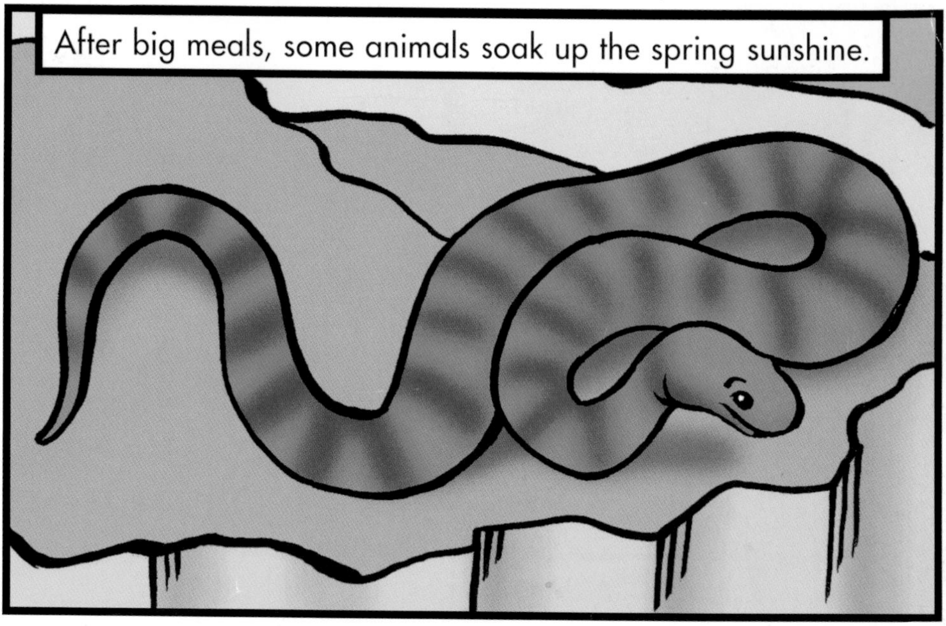
After big meals, some animals soak up the spring sunshine.

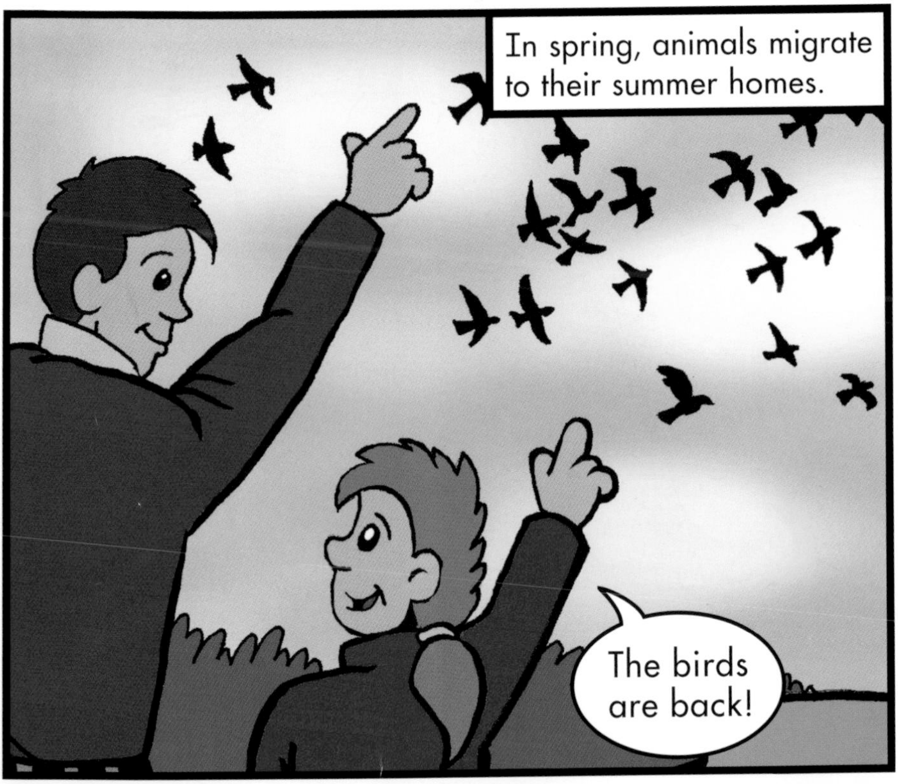
In spring, animals migrate to their summer homes.
The birds are back!

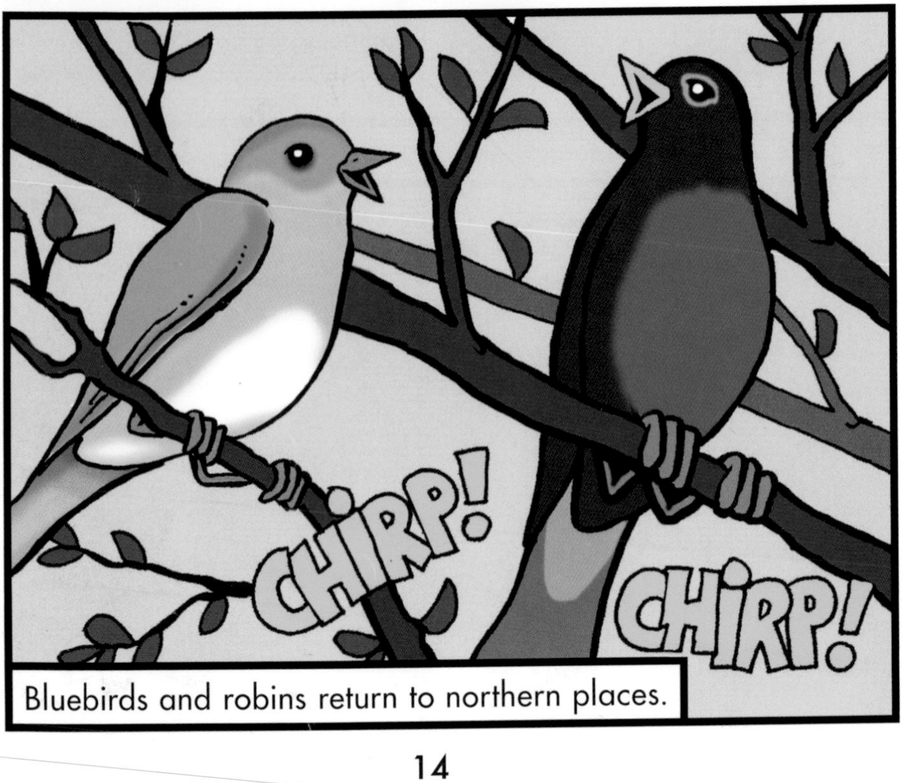
CHIRP!
CHIRP!
Bluebirds and robins return to northern places.

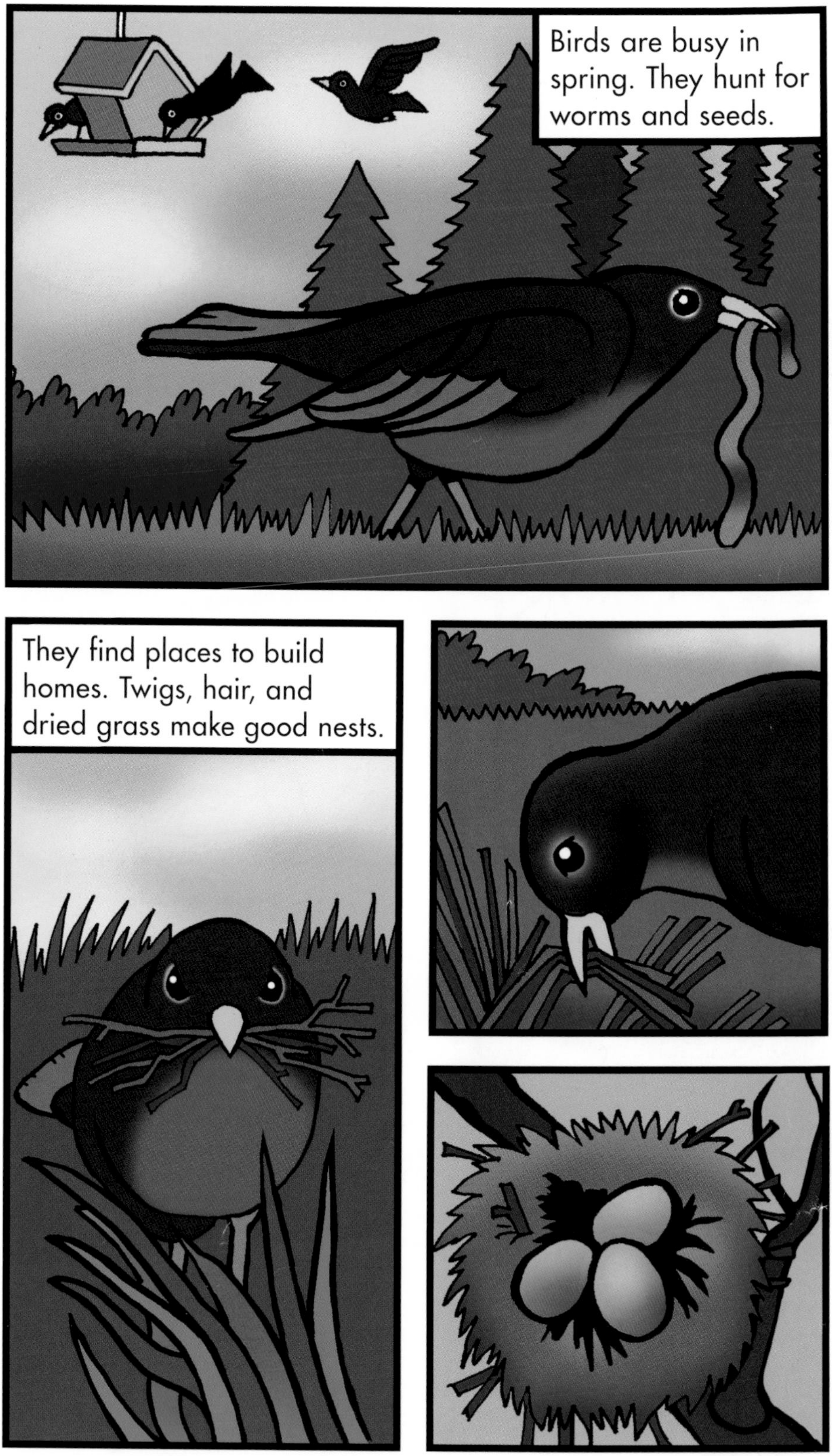
Birds are busy in spring. They hunt for worms and seeds.
They find places to build homes. Twigs, hair, and dried grass make good nests.

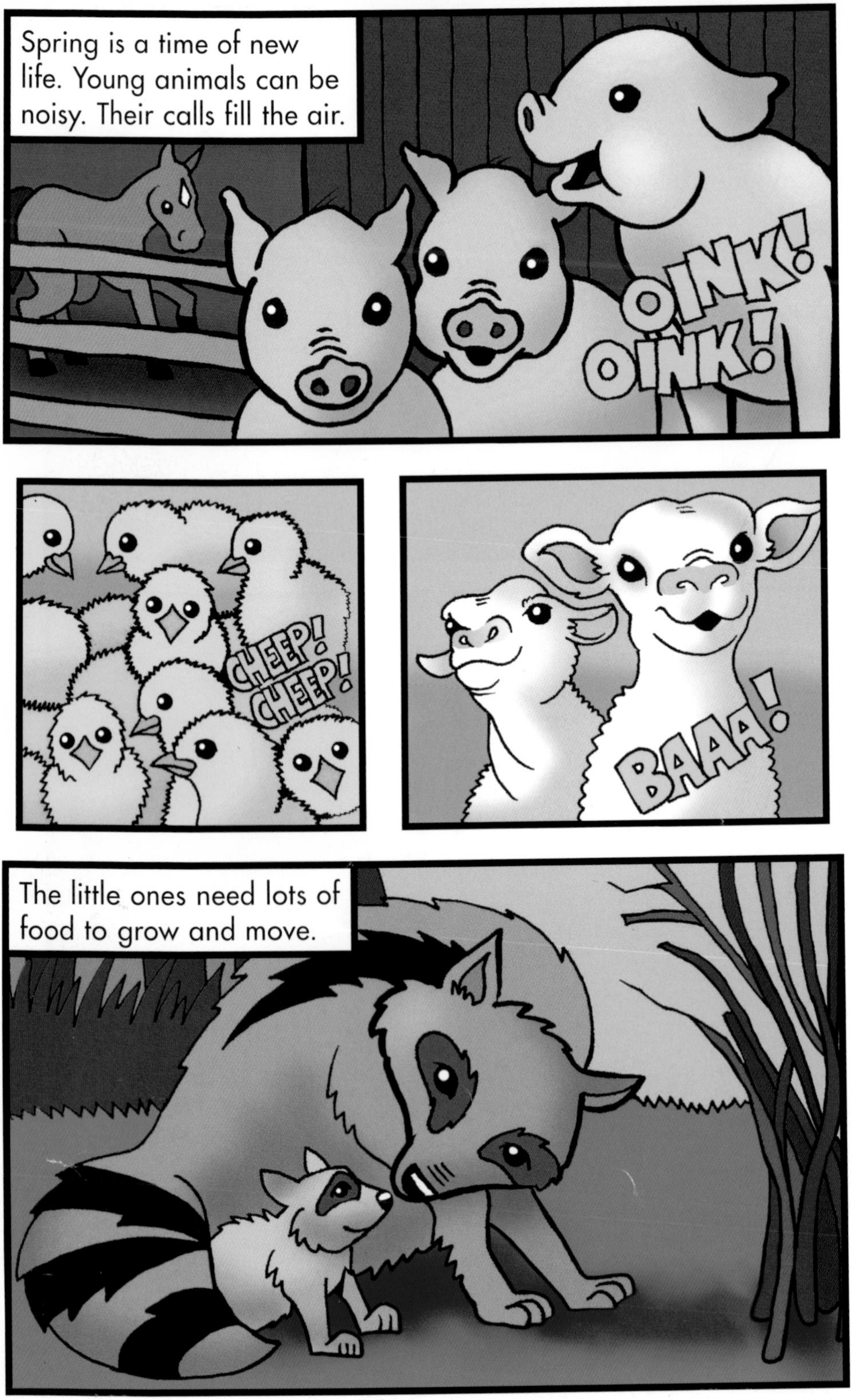
Spring is a time of new life. Young animals can be noisy. Their calls fill the air.
OINK! OINK!
CHEEP! CHEEP!
BAAA!
The little ones need lots of food to grow and move.

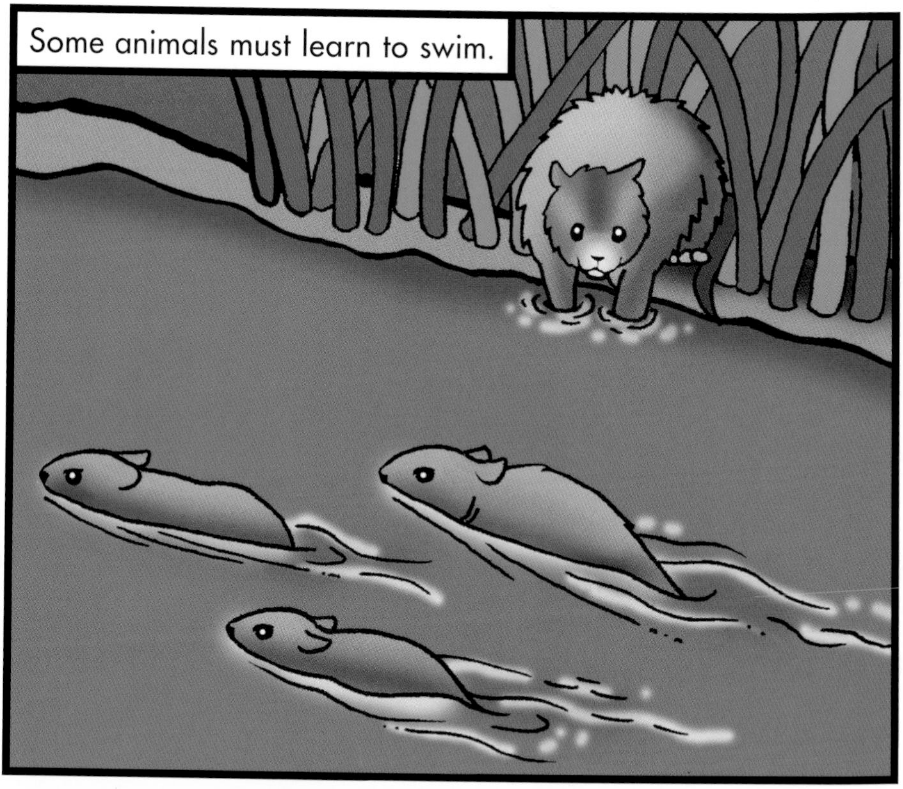
Some animals must learn to swim.

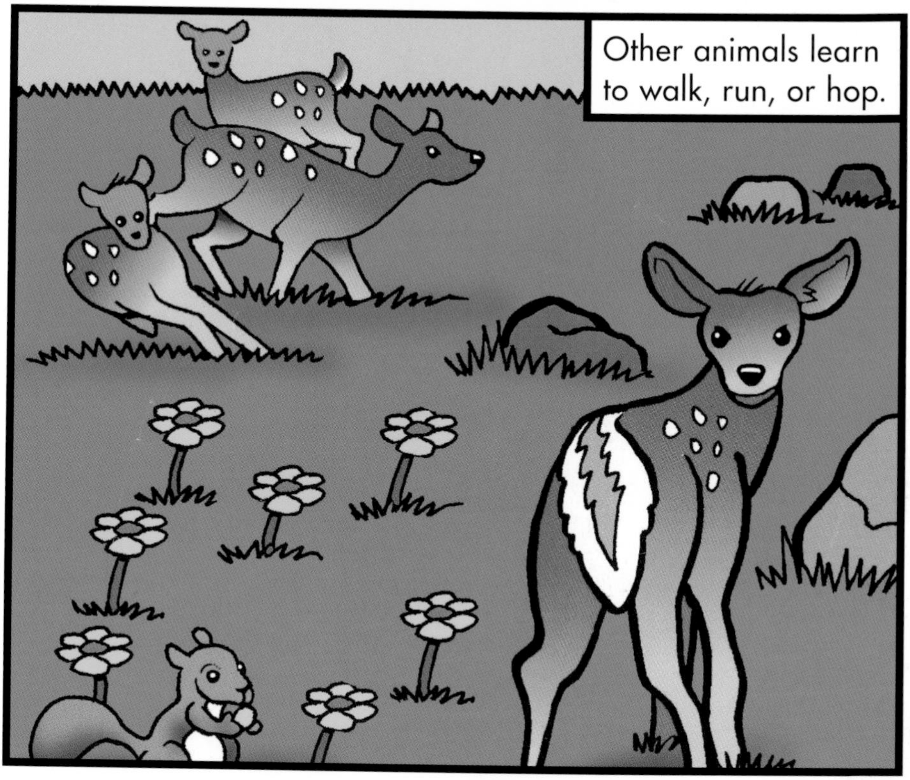
Other animals learn to walk, run, or hop.

SPRING FUN!

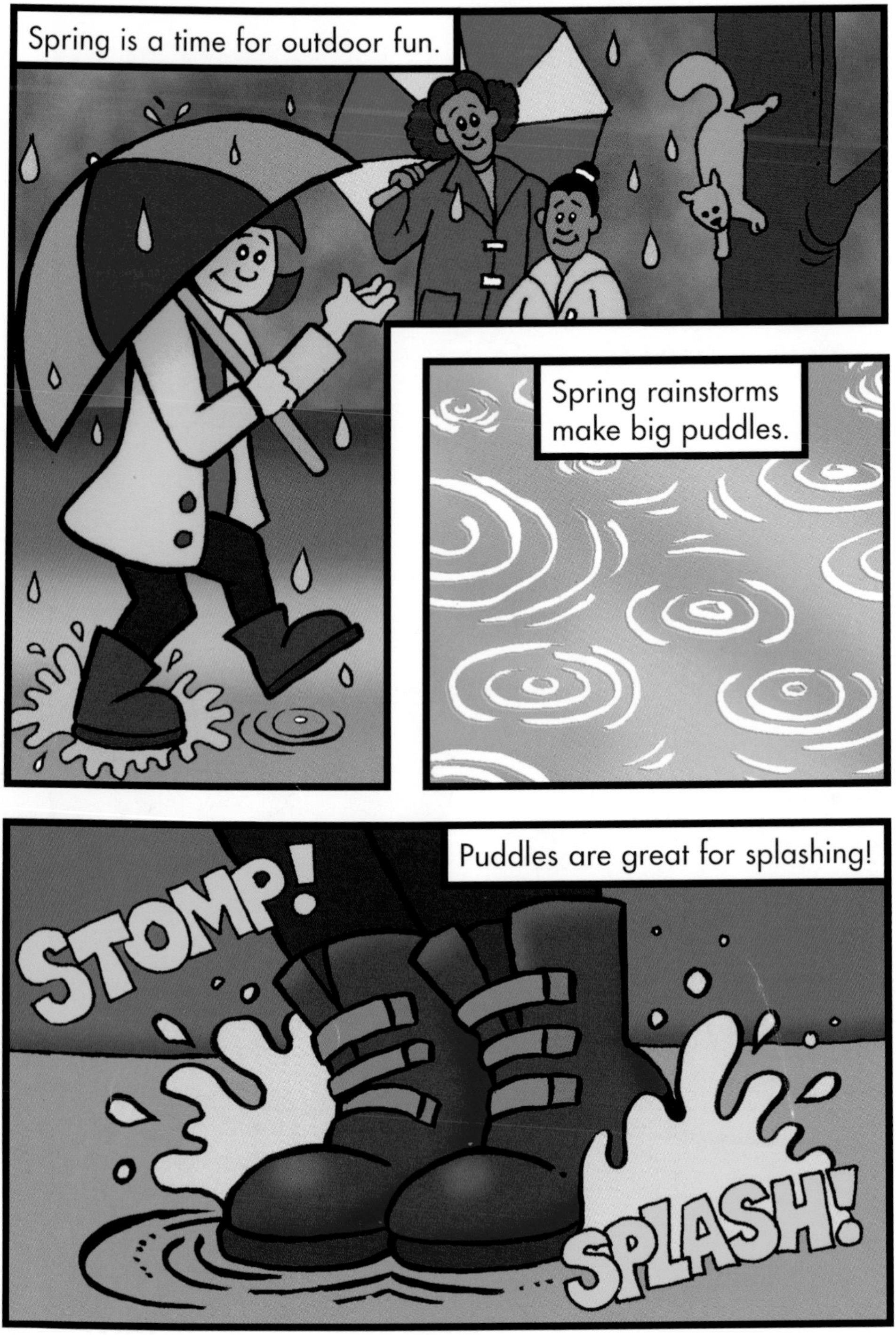
Spring is a time for outdoor fun.
Spring rainstorms make big puddles.
Puddles are great for splashing!
STOMP!
SPLASH!

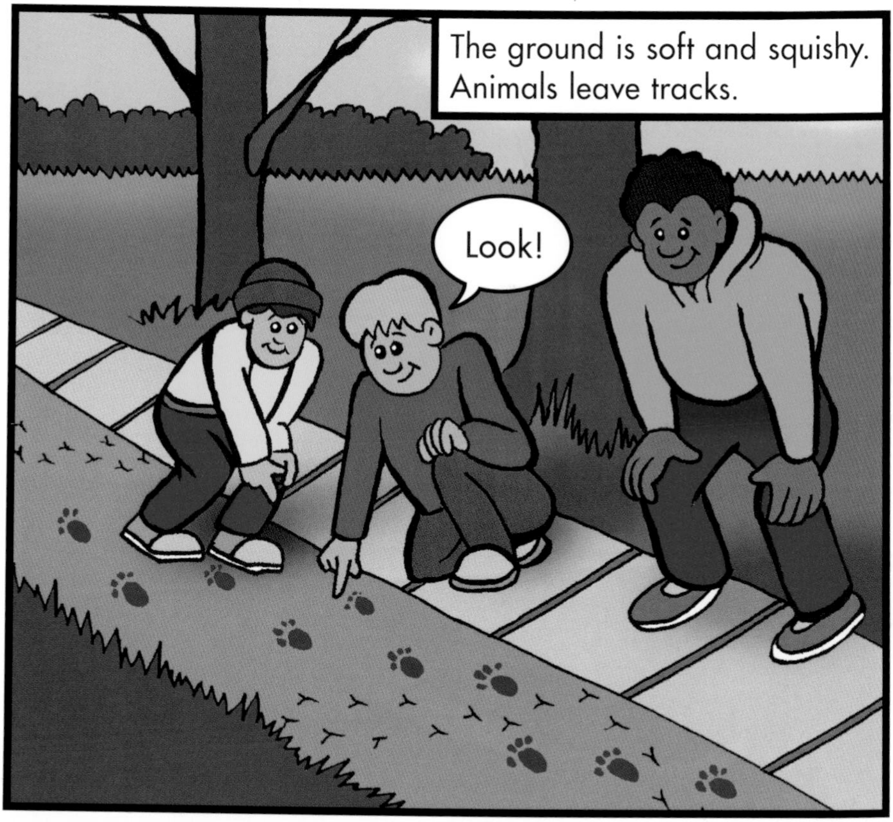
The ground is soft and squishy.
Animals leave tracks.
Look!

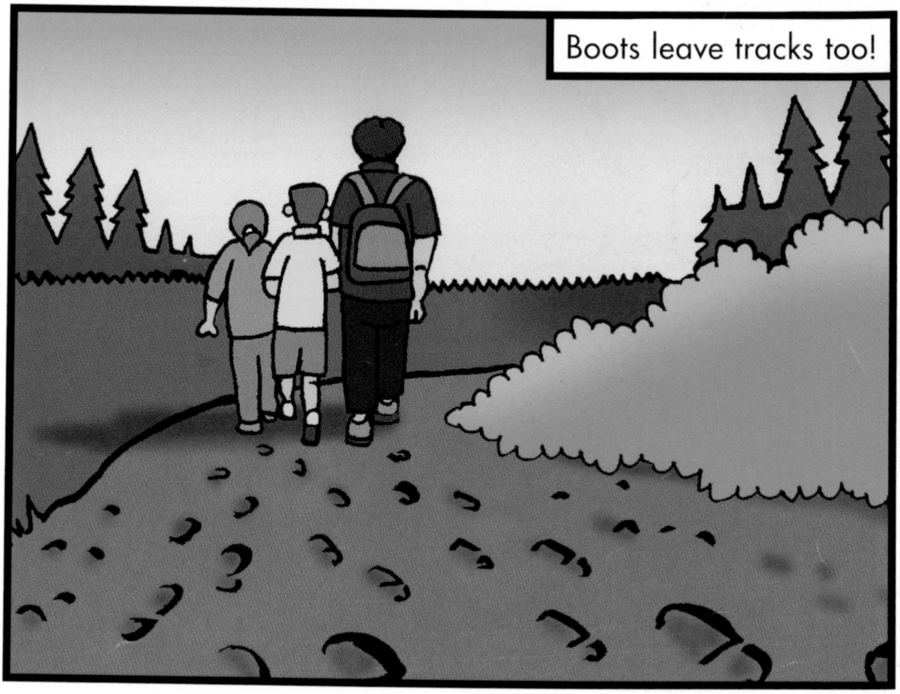
Boots leave tracks too!

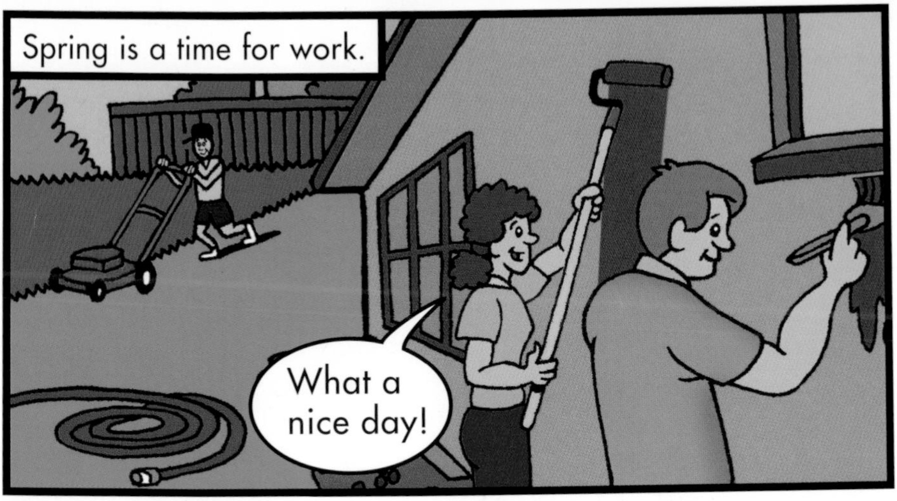
Spring is a time for work.
What a nice day!

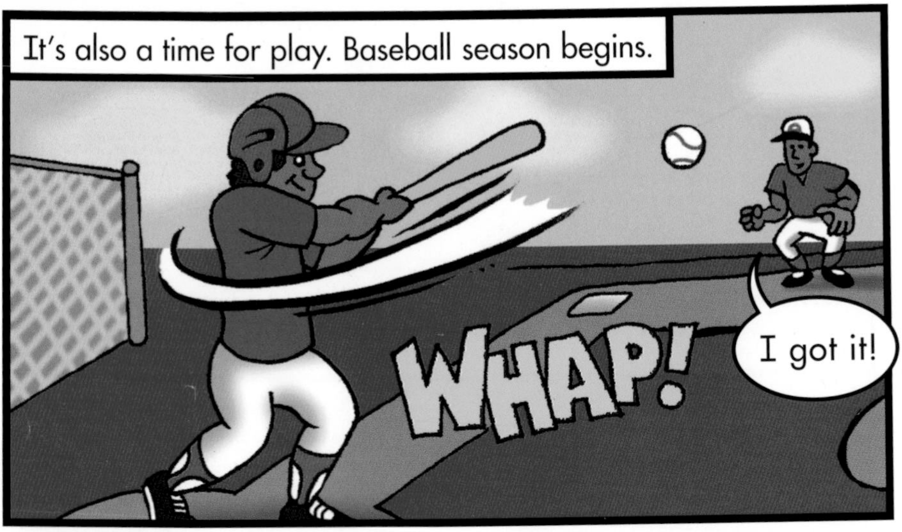
It's also a time for play. Baseball season begins.
WHAP!
I got it!

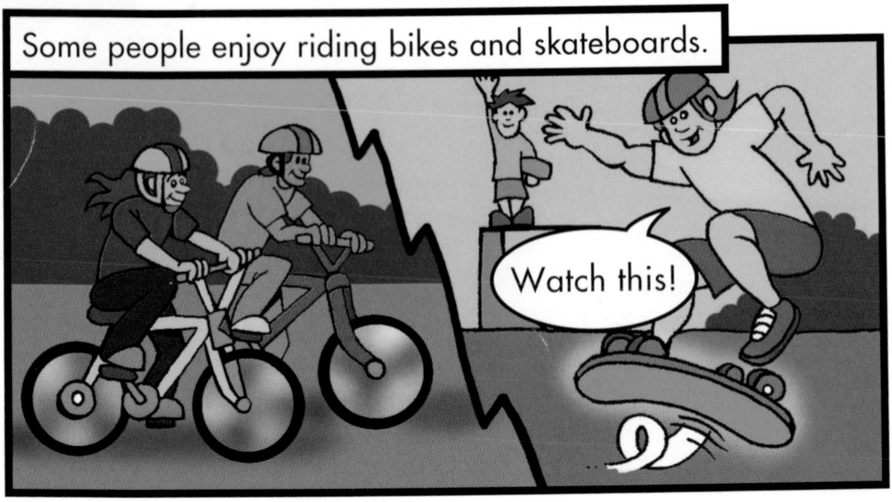
Some people enjoy riding bikes and skateboards.
Watch this!

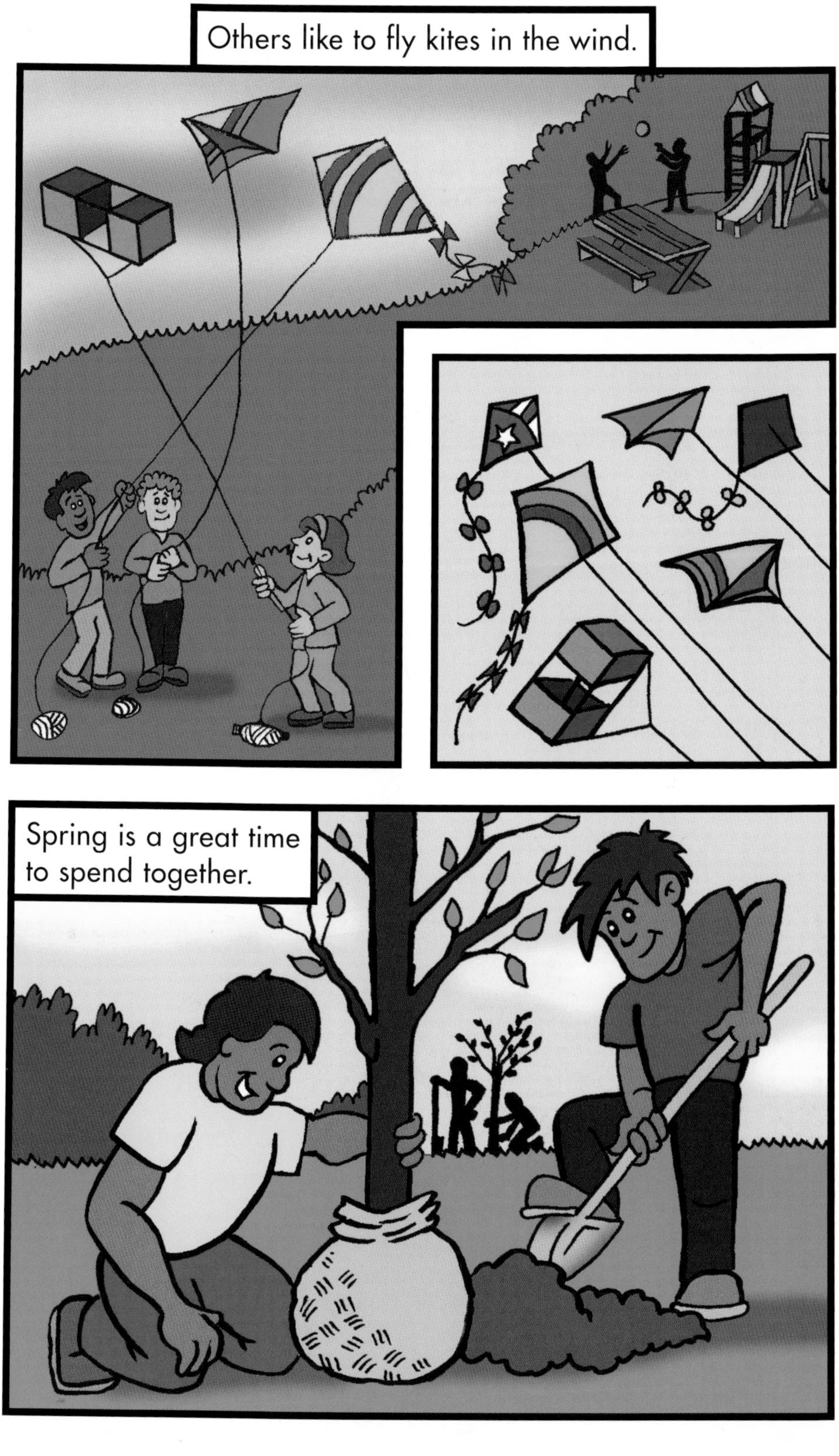
Others like to fly kites in the wind.
Spring is a great time to spend together.

GLOSSARY

angle—the figure formed by two lines or flat surfaces that extend from one point or line

axis—an imaginary line that runs through the middle of Earth from the North Pole to the South Pole

bud—the part of a plant that may become a flower

bulb—the onion-shaped underground plant part from which some plants grow

crop—a plant grown in large amounts; crops are usually grown for food

equator—an imaginary line around the middle of Earth; areas near the equator are usually warm and wet

hemisphere—one half of Earth

hibernate—to deeply sleep or rest quietly during winter

migrate—to move from one place to another when seasons change or food is hard to find

soil—another word for dirt

sprout—to start to grow

READ MORE

Emerson, Carl. *The Busy Spring.* Read-It! Readers: Science. Minneapolis: Picture Window Books, 2009.

Rotner, Shelley, and Anne Love Woodhull. *Every Season.* New Milford, Conn.: Roaring Brook Press, 2007.

Stewart, Melissa. *Why Do the Seasons Change?* Tell Me Why, Tell Me How. New York: Marshall Cavendish Benchmark, 2007.

INTERNET SITES

FactHound offers a safe, fun way to find Internet sites related to this book. All of the sites on FactHound have been researched by our staff.

Here's all you do:

Visit *www.facthound.com*

Type in this code: 9781429647298

INDEX

SEASONS

TITLES IN THIS SET:

FALL IS FUN

SPRING IS SPECIAL

SUMMER IS SUPER

WINTER IS WONDERFUL

FIRST GRAPHICS